Lazy Daisies of Summer

Grow an indoor garden of beautiful daisies! Juliana Schiweck's six lovely creations are easily reproduced on 10 mesh plastic canvas with embroidery floss. The fresh-picked projects include a trivet, table runner, napkin holder, welcome sign, and coaster set. There's also a versatile shelf topper that can be used to add color on tables, dressers, cabinets – anywhere you would like to see summer's sweetest blooms!

Trivet

Size: 7"w x 7"h (17.75cm x 17.75cm)

Supplies: DMC Embroidery Floss (refer to color key), one 10½" x 13½" (26.75cm x 34.25cm) sheet of clear 10 mesh plastic canvas, and #24 tapestry needle.

Instructions:

1. Follow chart to cut and stitch Trivet piece, using six strands of floss.
2. Using blue overcast stitches, cover unworked edges of trivet.

Napkin Holder

Size: 7"w x 7"h x 2¾"d (17.75cm x 17.75cm x 7cm)

Supplies: DMC Embroidery Floss (refer to color key), two 10½" x 13½" (26.75cm x 34.25cm) sheets of clear 10 mesh plastic canvas, and #24 tapestry needle.

Instructions:

1. Follow charts to cut and stitch Napkin Holder pieces, using six strands of floss.
2. Using blue overcast stitches, join Napkin Holder Front and Back to Napkin Holder Long Side.
3. Join Napkin Holder Front and Back to Napkin Holder Short Side.
4. Join Napkin Holder Bottom to Napkin Holder Front and Back, Napkin Holder Long Side, and Napkin Holder Short Side.
5. Cover remaining unworked edges of Napkin Holder.

Table Runner

Size: 21"w x 7"h (53.25cm x 17.75cm)

Supplies: DMC Embroidery Floss (refer to color key), three 10½" x 13½" (26.75cm x 34.25cm) sheets of clear 10 mesh plastic canvas, and #24 tapestry needle.

Instructions:

1. Follow chart to cut and stitch Table Runner pieces, using six strands of floss.
2. Referring to photo for placement, use blue overcast stitches to join Table Runner pieces.
3. Cover remaining unworked edges of Table Runner.

Trivet/Napkin Holder/Table Runner

(71 x 71 threads)

Cut and stitch one for Trivet.

Cut and stitch two for Napkin Holder.

Cut and stitch three for Table Runner.

KEY

COLOR (DMC)	COLOR (DMC)	COLOR (DMC)
white (3865)	lt lavender (211)	dk blue (336)
vy lt yellow (3823)	lavender (209)	vy lt green (472)
lt yellow (3078)	purple (340)	lt green (470)
yellow (743)	lt blue (3747)	green (3363)
gold (3852)	blue (792)	dk green (936)

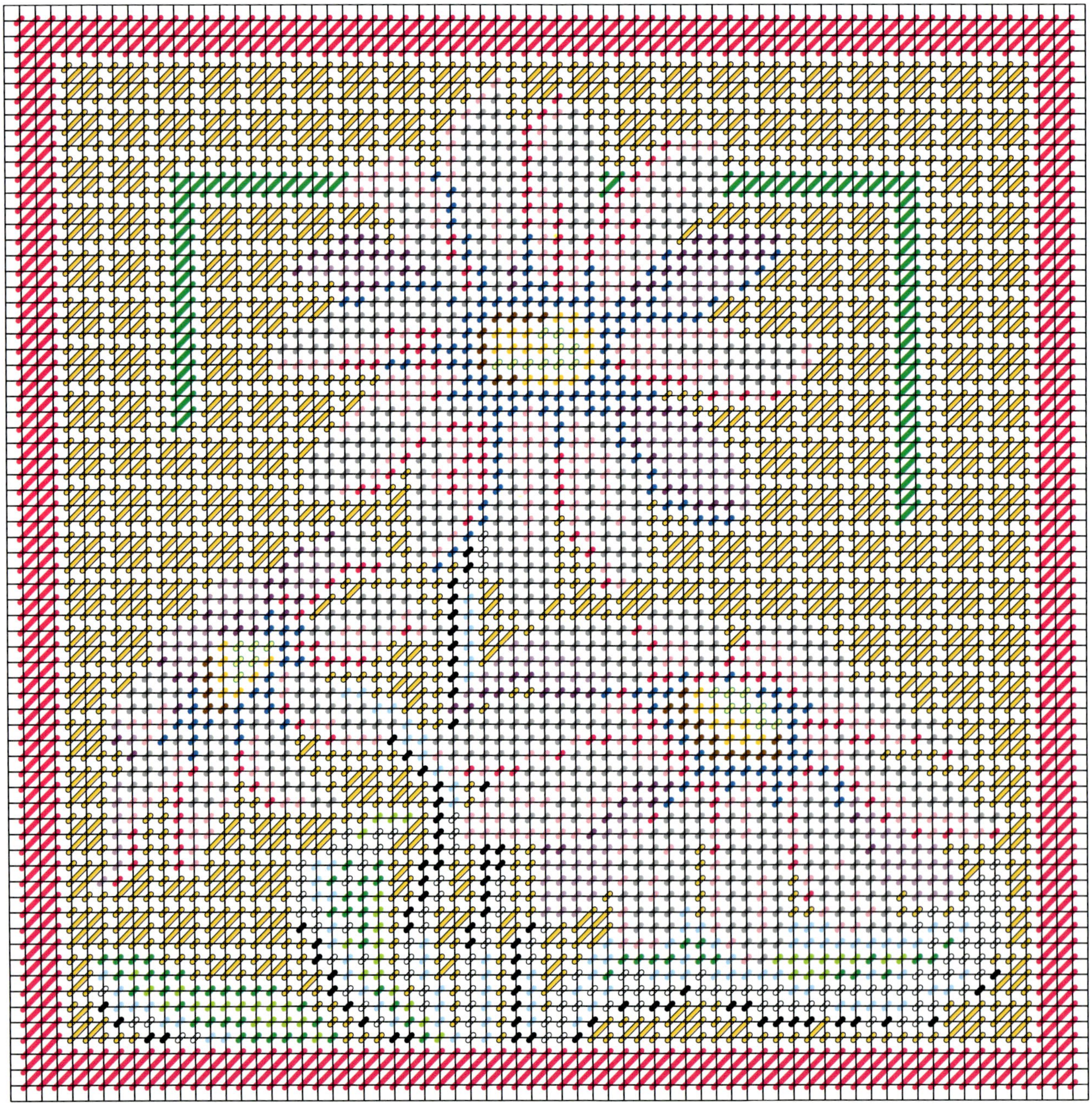

Napkin Holder Short Side

(26 x 32 threads)

Napkin Holder Long Side/Bottom

(26 x 71 threads) (stitch 2)

Coasters

Approx. Size: 4½"w x 5"h (11.5cm x 12.75cm) each

Supplies: DMC Embroidery Floss (refer to color key), one 10½" x 13½" (26.75cm x 34.25cm) sheet of clear 10 mesh plastic canvas, and #24 tapestry needle.

Instructions:

1. Follow charts to cut and stitch Coaster pieces, using six strands of floss.

KEY

COLOR (DMC)

- white (3865)
- vy lt yellow (3823)
- lt yellow (3078)
- yellow (743)
- gold (3852)
- lt lavender (211)
- lavender (209)
- purple (340)
- lt blue (3747)
- blue (792)
- dk blue (336)
- vy lt green (472)
- lt green (470)
- green (3363)
- dk green (936)

Coaster 1 (47 x 50 threads)

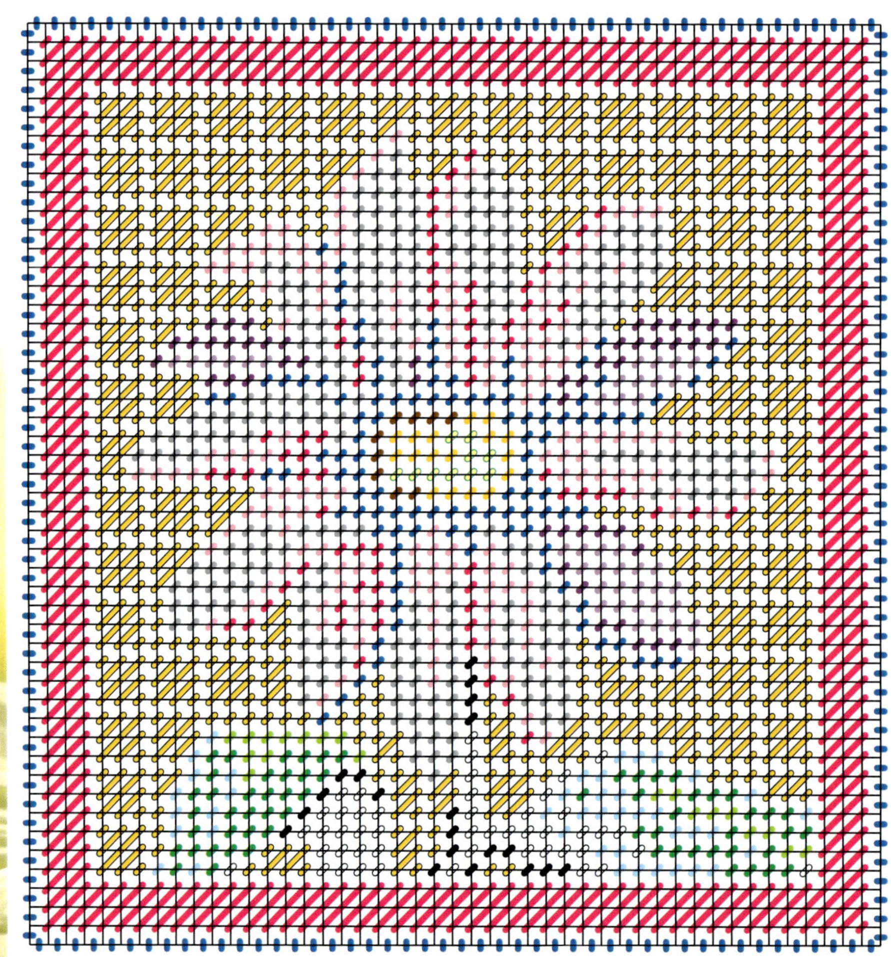

Coasters

Coaster 2 (50 x 47 threads)

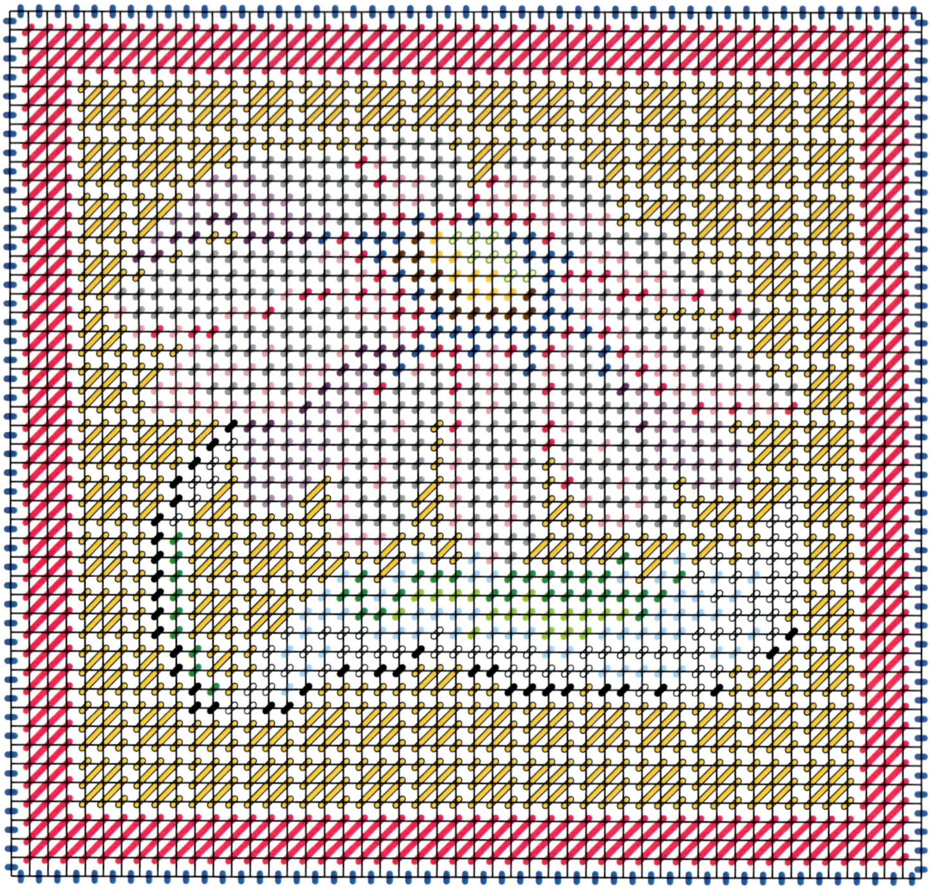

Coaster 3 (50 x 47 threads)

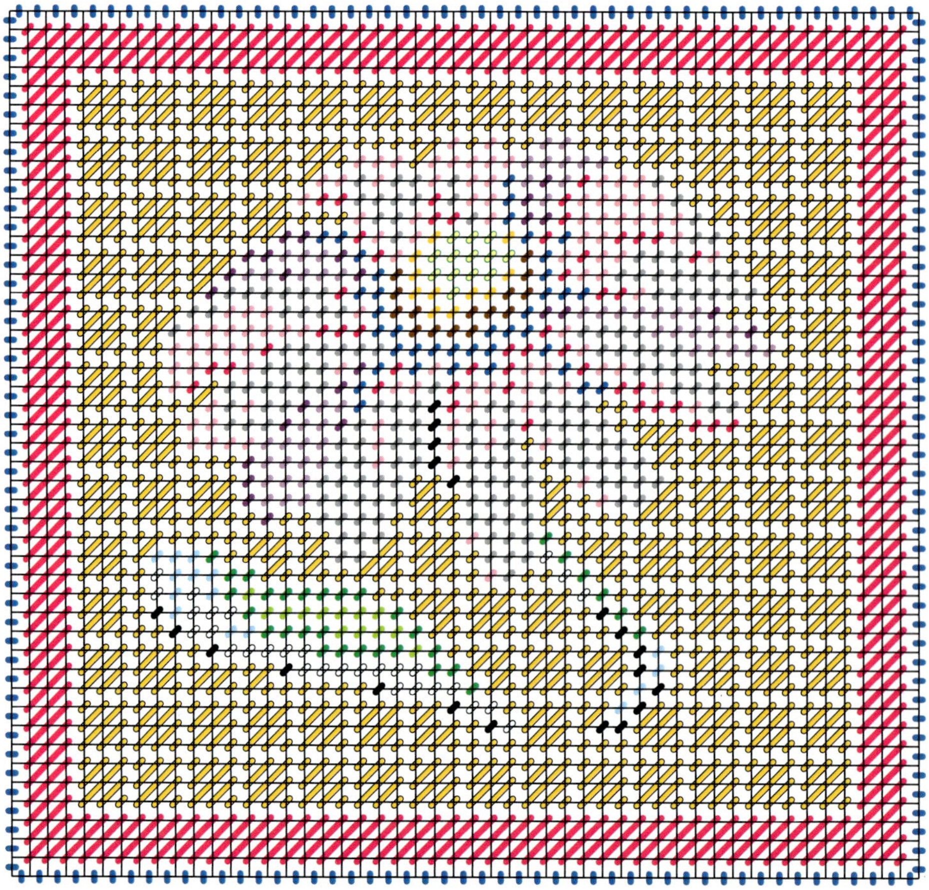

Welcome Sign

Size: 13½"w x 6½"h (34.25cm x 16.5cm)

Supplies: DMC Embroidery Floss (refer to color key), one 10½" x 13½" (26.75cm x 34.25cm) sheet of clear 10 mesh plastic canvas, and #24 tapestry needle.

Instructions:

1. Follow chart to cut and stitch Welcome Sign piece, using six strands of floss.

WELCOME

Welcome Sign

Welcome Sign (134 x 66 threads)

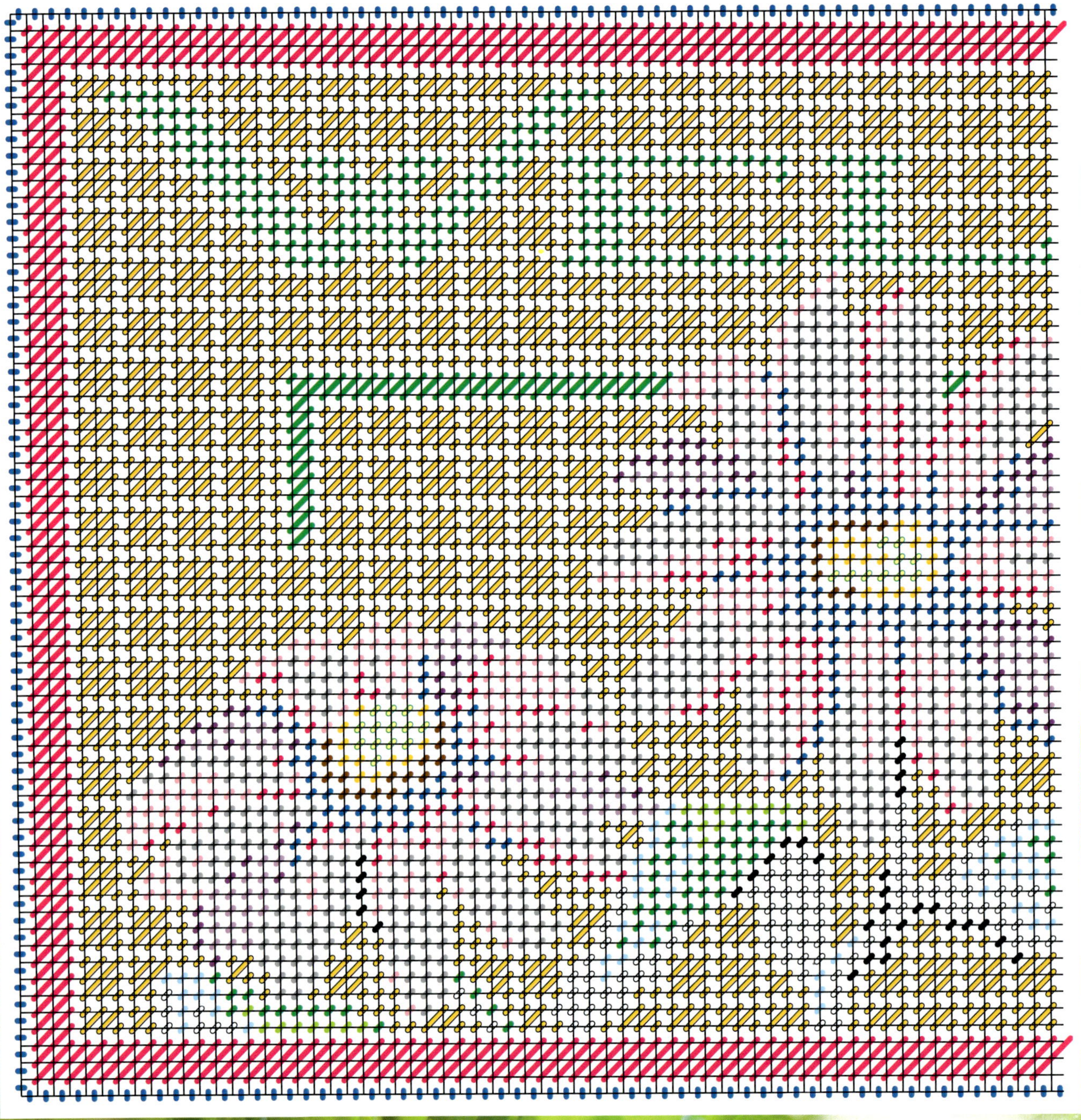

KEY

COLOR (DMC)	COLOR (DMC)	COLOR (DMC)
white (3865)	lt lavender (211)	dk blue (336)
vy lt yellow (3823)	lavender (209)	vy lt green (472)
lt yellow (3078)	purple (340)	lt green (470)
yellow (743)	lt blue (3747)	green (3363)
gold (3852)	blue (792)	dk green (936)

Chart Note: This chart of the Welcome Sign represents one 134 x 66 thread canvas piece. It is spread across two pages to make it large enough to be followed easily. No threads or stitches are repeated from one page to the next.

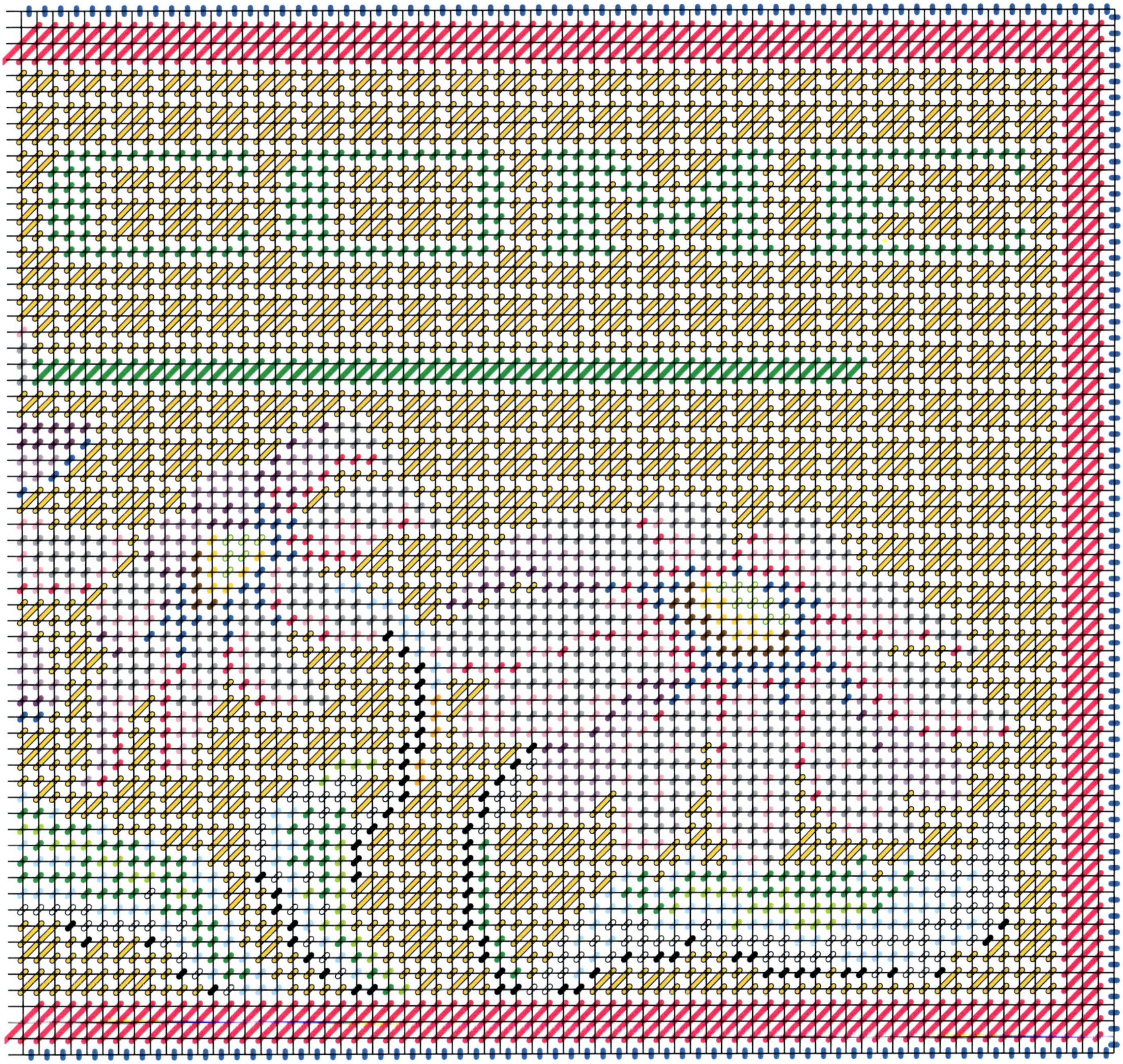

Shelf Topper

Approx. Size: 13½"w x 5¼"h (34.25cm x 13.25cm)

Supplies: DMC Embroidery Floss (refer to color key), one 10½" x 13½" (26.75cm x 34.25cm) sheet of clear 10 mesh plastic canvas, and #24 tapestry needle.

Instructions:

1. Follow charts to cut and stitch Coaster pieces, using six strands of floss.
2. Place on shelf as desired.

Shelf Topper

Shelf Topper (134 x 54 threads)

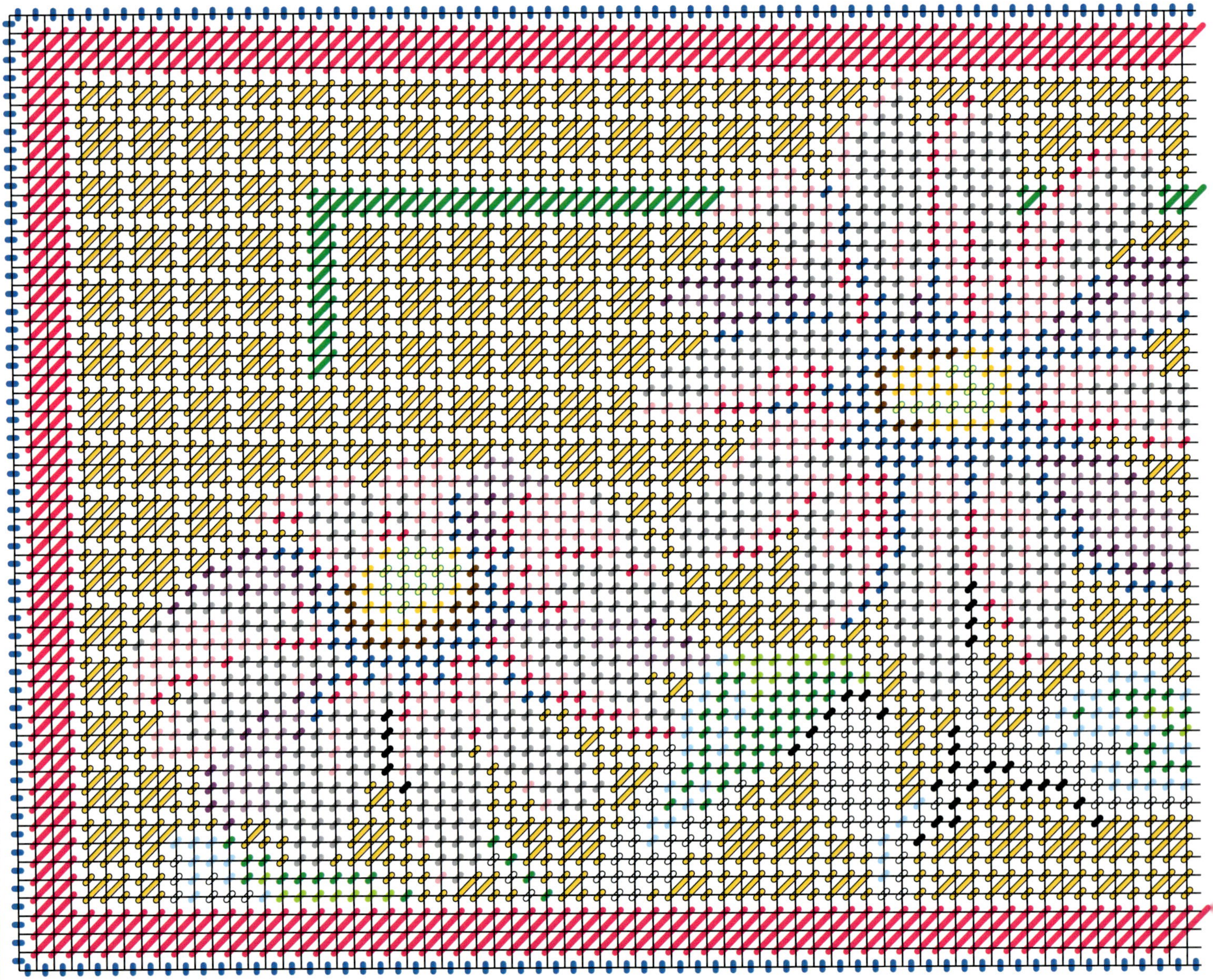

KEY

COLOR (DMC)	COLOR (DMC)	COLOR (DMC)
white (3865)	lt lavender (211)	dk blue (336)
vy lt yellow (3823)	lavender (209)	vy lt green (472)
lt yellow (3078)	purple (340)	lt green (470)
yellow (743)	lt blue (3747)	green (3363)
gold (3852)	blue (792)	dk green (936)

Chart Note: This chart of the Shelf topper represents one 134 x 54 thread canvas piece. It is spread across two pages to make it large enough to be followed easily. No threads or stitches are repeated from one page to the next.

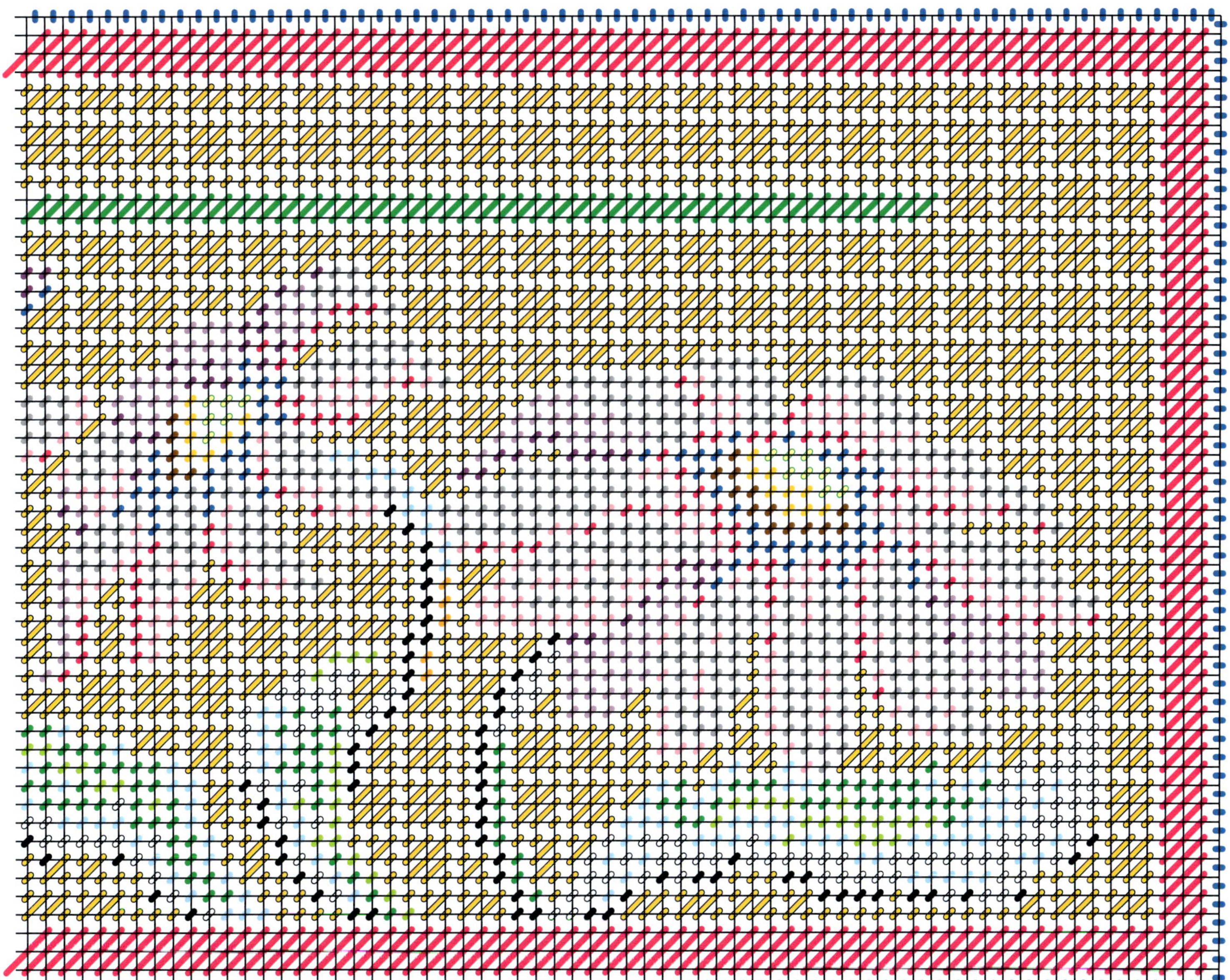

Plastic Canvas Basics

WORKING WITH PLASTIC CANVAS

Counting Threads. Throughout this leaflet, the lines of the canvas will be referred to as threads. However, they are not actually "threads" since the canvas is not woven. Before cutting out your pieces, note the thread count of each chart. The thread count is listed above the chart and indicates the number of threads in the width and height of the canvas pieces. To cut plastic canvas pieces accurately, count **threads** (not **holes**) as shown in **Fig. 1.**

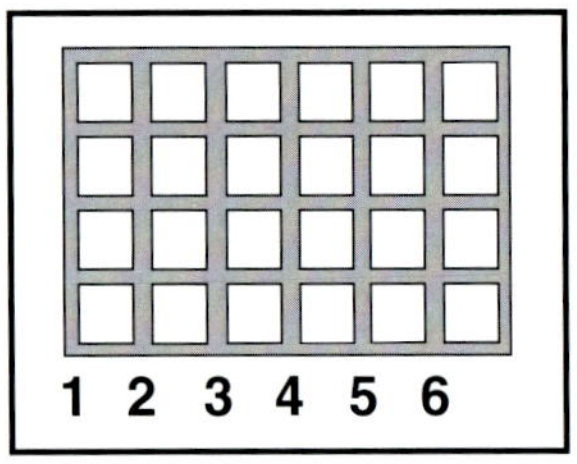

Fig. 1

Marking the Canvas. If you find it necessary to mark on the canvas, use an overhead projector pen. Outline shape with pen, cut out shape, and remove markings with water and a towel.

Cutting the Canvas. When cutting canvas, make sure to cut as close to the thread as possible without cutting into the thread. If you don't cut close enough, "nubs" or "pickets" will be left on the edge of your canvas. Make sure to cut all nubs from the canvas before you begin to stitch because nubs will snag the floss and are difficult to cover.

WORKING WITH EMBROIDERY FLOSS

Separating Floss Strands. DMC Embroidery Floss is used for the projects in this leaflet. Embroidery floss is made up of six strands that are twisted together. To ensure smoother stitches, separate strands and realign them before threading needle.

Dye Lot Variations. It is important to buy all of the floss you need to complete your project from the same dye lot. Although variations in color may be slight when flosses from two different dye lots are held together, the variation is usually apparent on a stitched piece.

READING THE COLOR KEY

A color key is included for each project. The heading in each color key is for the descriptive color name **(COLOR)** and for DMC Embroidery Floss **(DMC)**. The key indicates the colors of floss used and how each color is represented on the chart. For example, when white floss is represented by a grey line in the color key, all grey stitches on the chart should be stitched using white floss.

READING THE CHART

Whenever possible, the drawing on the chart looks like the completed stitch. For example, the tent stitches on the chart are drawn diagonally across one intersection of threads just like tent stitches look on your piece of canvas. If you have difficulty determining how a particular stitch is worked, refer to Stitch Diagrams.

STITCHING THE DESIGN

Securing the First Stitch. Don't knot the end of your floss before you begin stitching. Instead, begin each length of floss by coming up from the wrong side of the canvas and leaving a 1"- 2" (2.5cm x 5cm) tail on the wrong side. Hold this tail against the canvas and work the first few stitches over the tail. When secure, clip the tail close to your stitched piece. Clipping the tail closely is important because long tails can become tangled in future stitches or show through to the right side of the canvas.

Using Even Tension. Keep your stitching tension consistent, with each stitch lying flat and even on the canvas. Pulling or yanking the floss causes the tension to be too tight, and you will be able to see through your project. Loose tension is caused by not pulling the floss firmly enough, and the floss will not lie flat on the canvas.

Ending Your Stitches. After you've completed all of the stitches of one color in an area, end your stitching by running your needle under several stitches on the back of the stitched piece. To keep the tails of the floss from showing through or becoming tangled in future stitches, trim the end of the floss close to the stitched piece.

JOINING PIECES

Straight Edges. The most common method of assembling stitched pieces is joining two or more pieces of canvas along a straight edge using overcast stitches. Place one piece on top of the other with right or wrong sides together. Make sure the edges being joined are even, then stitch the pieces together through all layers.

Shaded Areas. The shaded area is part of a chart that has colored shading on top of it. Shaded areas usually mean that all the stitches in that area are used to join pieces of canvas. Don't work stitches in a shaded area until your project instructions say you should.

Stitching Tips

Length of Floss. It is best to begin stitching with a piece of floss that is approximately one yard (one meter) long. However, when working large areas of the same color, you may want to begin with a longer length of floss to reduce the number of ends and keep the back of your project looking neat.

Keeping Stitches Smooth. Most stitches tend to twist the floss. Drop your needle and let the floss untwist every few stitches or whenever needed.

Stitch Diagrams

Unless otherwise indicated, bring threaded needle up at **1** and all **odd** numbers and down at **2** and all **even** numbers.

TENT STITCH

This stitch is worked in horizontal and vertical rows over one intersection as shown in **Fig. 2.**

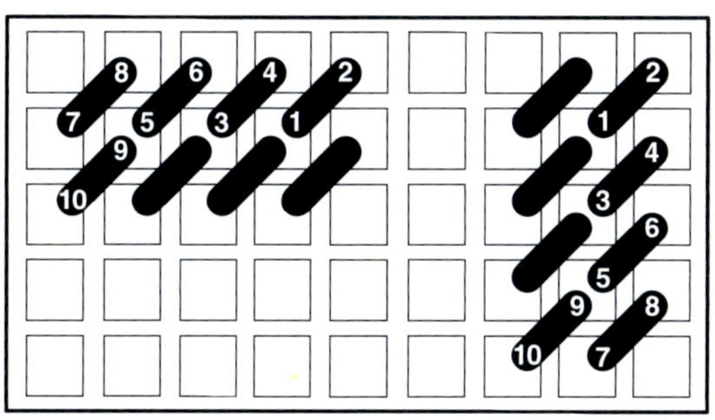

Fig. 2

GOBELIN STITCH

This basic straight stitch is worked over two or more threads or intersections **(Fig. 3).** The number of threads or intersections may vary according to the chart.

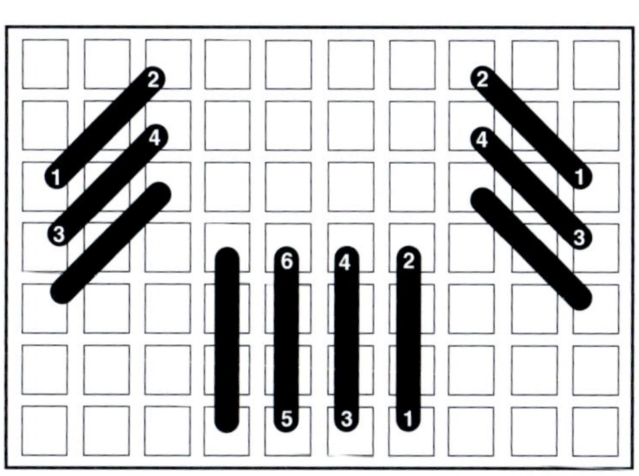

Fig. 3

SCOTCH STITCH

This basic stitch may be worked over three or more threads and forms a square. **Fig. 4** shows the Scotch stitch worked over three threads.

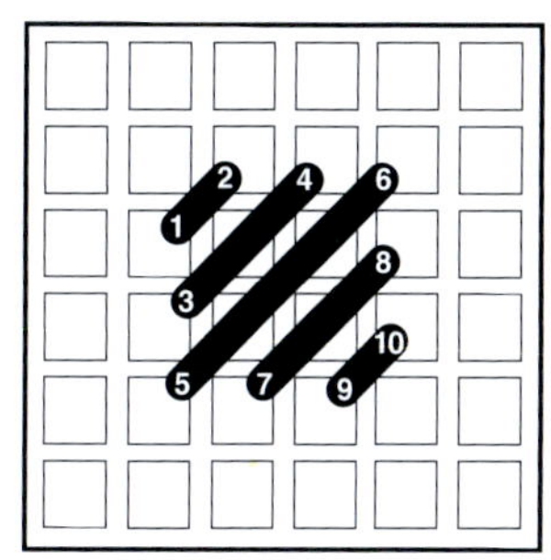

Fig. 4

OVERCAST STITCH

This stitch covers the edge of the canvas and joins pieces of canvas **(Fig. 5).** It may be necessary to go through the same hole more than once to get even coverage on the edge, especially at the corners.

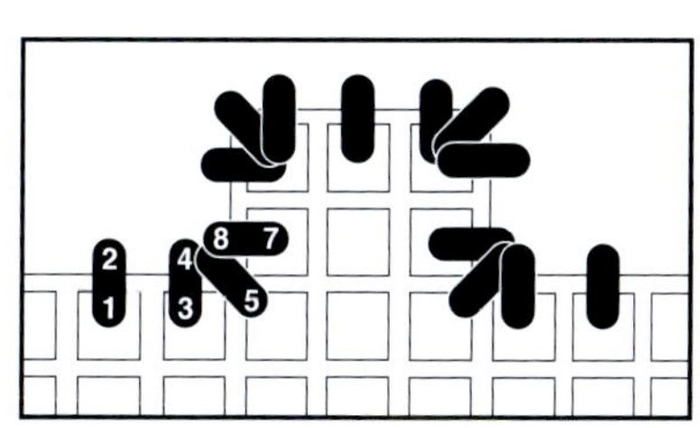

Fig. 5

Show us what you're working on!

Share your project photos with us on social media.
Tag us @leisureartsinc or use #leisurearts

Production Team: Publishing Manager - Megan Copeland; Technical Editor - Lisa Lancaster; Lead Graphic Artist - Michael Puckett; Graphic Artist - DeRosia Price-Webb; Photographer - Rob Karman; and Photo Stylist - Lori Wenger.

We have made every effort to ensure that these instructions are accurate and complete. We cannot, however, be responsible for human error, typographical mistakes, or variations in individual work.

Made in U.S.A.